HORRORSCOPE®

HORRORSCOPE®

by OLSON & KELSO

This 1992 edition is published by
Longmeadow Press
201 High Ridge Road
Stamford, CT 06904

ISBN: 0-681-41165-1

Printed in United States of America

0   9   8   7   6   5   4   3

So you want to know the future...

Do you ever read your daily horoscope and wonder what it **REALLY** means?

Well, don't worry, we've taken all the wonder out—completely out!

You see, it's all in the interpretation. As the great Irish philosopher **MURPHY** once said, if anything can go wrong, **IT WILL**. It's inevitable.

IT'S WRITTEN IN THE STARS!

Susan Kelso & Eric Olson

"You'll receive citation in recognition of behaviour."

Big things are coming your way. Be prepared for a change in lifestyle.

What goes around comes around.

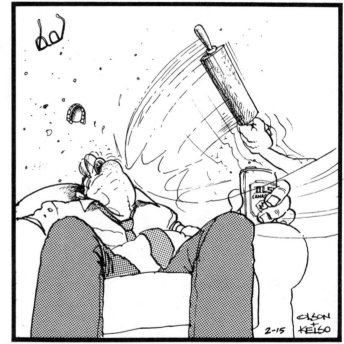

Romantic relationship is on the upswing.

You will be given an opportunity to hear both sides of an argument.

Others will be instrumental in helping you lose that excess baggage you've been carrying.

Skilled professional plays key role in opening doors for you.

Keep your mind on your work and you'll surely go places!

You could be overcome by the majesty of nature.

**"Your ability to get to the bottom of things
will be noted. Aries figures prominently."**

**Creative juices flow. You can finally say
'It's finished!'**

What seemed lost will magically reappear.

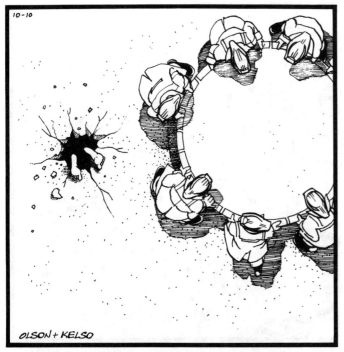

There will be times when you'll wish you had a wider circle of friends.

A slip of the tongue could land you in hot water.

You find it easy to trim your waistline in time for the holidays.

"Romance takes an interesting turn."

Finding a quiet setting at work will eliminate unnecessary interruptions.

Today you will have an opportunity to rise above it all!

"You may find that you are more sensitive than you thought."

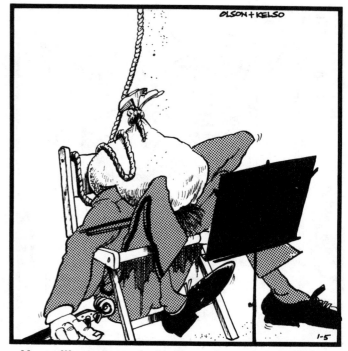

You will never again have to play second fiddle.

You will see things from a new perspective today.

Today will be very similar to yesterday.

"Your efforts will be rewarded with
cold, hard cash."

"A blind date will be studded with excitement."

"This is your power day."

"You'll be in really good spirits this evening."

Distance barriers will eventually disappear. Very soon you will be able to communicate face to face.

You see a situation from a different perspective today. It comes to you in a blinding flash.

A date is impressed by your style and your dash.

Credit and loan applications will get a quick response.

There's nothing like a roaring fire to help you relax and clear your head.

Get down to nitty-gritty paperwork before key meetings. Management will be quick to take notice of your ability to prepare.

Your current career status will be in for change. You will reach new heights.

An unexpected turn of events could leave you with stars in your eyes.

All signals are go for launching a pet project.

Today you receive help in extinguishing an inflamed situation.

**You get important thoughts on paper.
You're really on a roll!**

Person who carries weight is now on your side.

Home repairs are on tap today. You seem to have all bases covered!

Be cautious in the car today. A seat belt could save your neck.

You get a head start on household chores today.

A small child gives you a new spring in your step.

You find you are getting more out of life than in the past.

You have the ability to see through complicated news issues.

A big fan of yours will drop in unexpectedly today.

Evening features short trip – love lights the way!

Your career will take you down a new path.

Co-worker helps you clear your cluttered desk.

Lunar position brings out the sensitive side of you.

You've got what it takes to make even more great gains today.

Fitness goals are within reach if you have what it takes to get there.

Try not to lose your train of thought today. Concentrate on what lies ahead and you'll stay on track.

You and your mate will successfully patch up your differences today.

Rush hour traffic won't be a problem this morning.

A vexing task is easier if you break it into smaller parts.

The written word helps you get to the bottom of things.

You receive help with out of pocket expenses.

Your mate will display true feelings of love.

A step-by-step approach will get you rolling much quicker today.

A breakthrough comes when you least expect it.

A tight-knit relationship is featured on this special day.

A great day for gathering information.

Romance will remain in a holding pattern.

A business trip to a new destination is a strong possibility.

A break in routine chores could leave you feeling bubbly all over.

Those in authority feel you've got what they've been looking for. Now is the time to show them your stuff!

Steering clear of opposition will allow you to chart your own course.

Today you could be overcome by a moving musical experience.

You could be thinking, "It's true. My cup runneth over!"

The element of surprise gets things done at work.

Today you get a foot in the door with a new business venture.

Now you can say, 'I am in the driver's seat!'

Children will do much to brighten your life this evening.

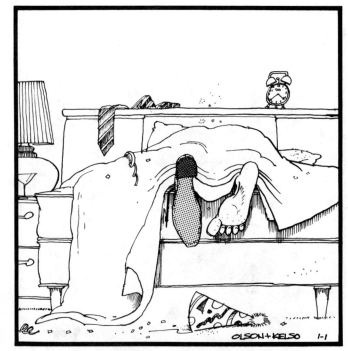

Avoid making any rash moves today. It's probably best to stay put and think things out.

An afternoon encounter will sweep you off your feet and leave your head spinning!

You'll get unexpected opportunity for some window shopping.

You finally get that 'big break' you deserve.

OLSON + KELSO

Get ready for big changes!

By maintaining a stern approach, you will continue to hold the reigns of authority.

Today you will find the proverbial pot at the end of the rainbow.

You make a big splash at a social event.

A friend will help you get to the bottom of things.

OLSON + KELSO

Be alert when dealing with sensitive issues.

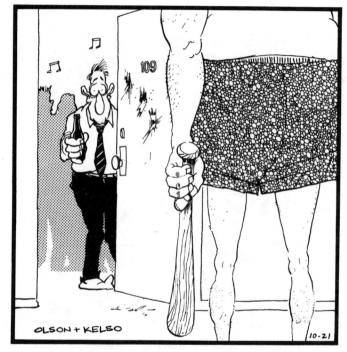

Your vibes are reaching people you don't even know.

Family ties will strengthen during the holiday season.

Things will roll your way if you lower your guard.

You could have a real breakthrough in your career.

You have a knack for getting people to open up.

"Romance sizzles with new heat!"

Cutting corners will be on your mind for most of the day.

"You have an uncanny ability to always look on the bright side."

"You're on your way to the top very quickly; enjoy the ride!"

You could be rubbing elbows with some real heavyweights.

"Doors that have been closed to you swing open."

You could pull off a grand slam today.

Evening will focus on late dining with member of the opposite sex.

Friends you've been dying to see will visit you soon.

A surprise is in store for you. What was lost will be recovered.

Things will be unusually active at work today.

If something is bothering you, get it off your chest.

Excitement and togetherness are part of the scenario today.

Today it will seem like everything you touch turns to gold!

**A good day to put your best foot forward.
You'll recover lost article.**

"There is no limit to how far you can go today."

Much that occurs is behind the scenes. A friendly greeting leaves you feeling on top of the world.

"Money is on your mind for a number of reasons."

Someone solicits your assistance in getting a major job off the ground. Roll up your sleeves and dig right in!

By digging beneath the surface, you'll uncover hidden source of power.

"Scenario features travel, refreshments and fine dining."

"Be wary of establishing too low a profile at work."

**"You feel more relaxed about
a new relationship."**

You are successful in diversifying your assets.

You find it easy to spot things quickly today.

A part-time job could lead to a long-term commitment.

You're riding high and no one can stop you!

Younger family member could develop interest in water sports.

Someone close to you will orchestrate a quick way to beat the system.

Spend time examining one of life's great mysteries.

You find a novel solution to a nagging problem.

You will come through with flying colors today.

A windfall could mean excitement and change of residence.

This may be a good day to try your hand at cooking something different.

A school reunion brings back lost memories.

There's definitely a light at the end of the tunnel.

OLSON + KELSO

8-11

You might be saying, "I've changed my mind and I feel good about it."

5-20

"Taurus figures prominently."

A new pet forms close attachment.

You are always able to adjust and fit in so well.

An unexpected practical joke will leave you in stitches!

What you have been waiting for is now upon you.

You discover that you can stay home and still have a ball.

A pot of gold could appear right under your nose.

OLSON + KELSO

You can look forward to a holiday void of all pressure.

Binding situation eases – you'll be free to roam.

You will break new ground.

You find exactly where you stand in connection with employment.

If you remain assertive, you are sure to get what's coming to you.

You have more in common with others than you'd imagined.

Today you could be thinking you've got it all!

Your ability to balance many facts and figures will leave a big impression on the boss!

You will hold the link to many new friendships today.

Your generosity will be appreciated by those who count.

Seize an opportunity to blow your own horn!

You may find yourself appealing to an influential woman today. Could involve long-term courting.

**A business trip will bring startling results.
Big bucks will seem to come out of nowhere.
You can't miss!**

You could run across an old friend today.

You have a knack for getting others to follow your lead.

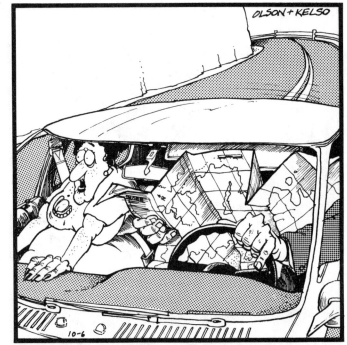

Reading material will assist you in dealing with a difficult situation head on.

You will be the focus of a secret admirer.

This will be a good day to make the rounds.

Get away this weekend and embrace the great outdoors. Blaze new trails!

Domestic scene highlighted. It's time to enjoy some remodeling.

Management will notice your ability to stay relaxed in high-pressure meetings.

This could be a good day to clear the deck and take in a movie.

You feel like you're walking on air today.

Your day will start off with a bang!

You will be feeling right up to scratch today.

Although you feel like you're dragging your heels, you really are in the fast lane.

OLSON + KELSO

SALE

11-23

Treat yourself to some shopping. It could provide you with the lift you need.

OLSON + KELSO 11-19

You begin to realize the benefit of staying in school.

Tackle paperwork early and you'll be able to knock off a little sooner than usual today.

Your career offers the chance to pick up great insight into the lives of others.

An afternoon stroll in the park could help you relax and unwind.

Things will really start to heat up today. You'll say, "Now we're cooking!"

Today you could be thinking, "If the shoe fits, wear it!"

A good day to enjoy an outing – go with the flow.

Today is your power day.

Someone will make you an offer you can't refuse.

A period of tough sledding comes to an end.

Financial security is on the way. You'll be feeling safe very soon now.

You'll face the day with a full head of steam.

You have what it takes to move forward in your career. Press on!

OLSON + KELSO

12-18

A recent stock purchase will produce big returns!

OLSON + KELSO

12-24

You will be showered with unexpected gifts.

Today you will feel free as a bird.

Your business day gets off to a running start.

You will always have a close friend by your side.

"Those who said it couldn't be done will now admit, 'You did it'."

"A good day to strengthen relationship with neighbours."

"If you take a look around, you will see just how well you are doing."

"Suddenly, friends appear. Popularity increases."

"You will appreciate the strong ties
of a friend today."

"You discover a major breakthrough."

"Your firm grasp of things enables you to move forward at a steady pace."

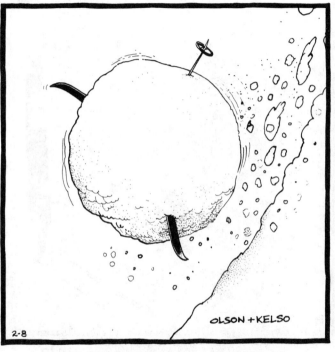

"You're likely to declare, 'Nothing can stop me now!'"

"You may find others very demanding at work today."

"After overcoming many obstacles, you are now in the spotlight."

"You will have an opportunity to make a lasting impression today. Be on your toes."

"Focus on paperwork before going out tonight."

"A wish to work in theatre will be fulfilled."

"A burden is lifted."

**"Your ability to keep a level head
will help you excel today."**

"What begins as emotional conflagration will end up with peace and tranquility."

"Those who love you are behind you all the way."

"You will climb corporate ladder."

"Popularity zooms upwards."

**"You could be saying, 'I found it
and it's mine!'"**

**"Others find your good taste most satisfying.
Leo involved."**

"You will meet a tall, dark stranger."

"You will be well situated in your work today."

"You get a chance to start over."

"Money that had been withheld will
be released."

"A new partnership adds zest to your life.
You continue to thrive on change."

"Children will be helpful in surprising ways."

You have a special air about you.

Your enthusiasm for activity is almost limitless today.

"Someone might ask 'where have you been keeping those hidden charms?'."

Be discreet while looking for a way out of your current situation. You may need to go under cover to investigate.

Things will fall your way when you turn over a new leaf.

You will finally have your name in lights.

Today you will earn your stripes!

Plan to take some time off – you deserve it.

Today it is definitely hats off to you!

Your career is picking up.

Aquarian is featured.

What had been missing will resurface.

"A golden opportunity may be right at your feet."

"Today you will awake feeling like a kid again."

You have a knack for getting people to help you out.

"A long distance journey is on the horizon."

"You will experience a stroke of good fortune this evening."

A new career could see you going in many directions at once.

"You will be able to really let yourself go when you discover there are 'no strings attached'."

"Your outgoing personality and ability to deal with the public will finally bear fruit."

"There are fewer things to tie you down now. Rejoice!"

"Co-worker will give you a hand today."

"A little recreation will leave you feeling like a king. Mate involved."

"A close friend will have you for dinner."

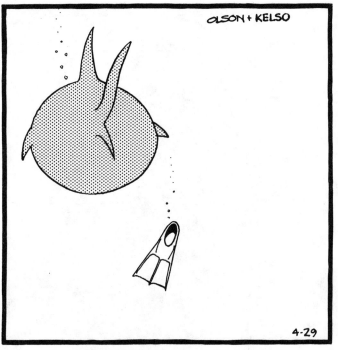

"Pisces figures prominently."

"The sun will shine on you and brighten up your day."

"Ball is in your court."

"Today will start off with an interesting twist."

"Your driving ability will leave a lasting impression."

"A brief encounter will take you by surprise."

"Confirm partnership agreements in advance."

"Getting about today will be a breeze."

Participating in sports will help ease tension.

No matter what happens, you will have the support of your friends.